WINNING
DIVORCE
STRATEGIES

WINNING DIVORCE STRATEGIES

*Intelligent and Aggressive Representation
for Every Person Going through Divorce or Custody
Proceedings in the State of New York*

Brian D. Perskin, Esq.

iUniverse, Inc.
Bloomington

Winning Divorce Strategies
Intelligent and Aggressive Representation for Every Person Going through
Divorce or Custody Proceedings in the State of New York

iUniverse books may be ordered through booksellers or by contacting:

iUniverse
1663 Liberty Drive
Bloomington, IN 47403
www.iuniverse.com
1-800-Authors (1-800-288-4677)

Because of the dynamic nature of the Internet, any web addresses or links contained in this book may have changed since publication and may no longer be valid. The views expressed in this work are solely those of the author and do not necessarily reflect the views of the publisher, and the publisher hereby disclaims any responsibility for them.

Any people depicted in stock imagery provided by Thinkstock are models, and such images are being used for illustrative purposes only.
Certain stock imagery © Thinkstock.

ISBN: 978-1-4759-5684-9 (sc)
ISBN: 978-1-4759-5686-3 (hc)
ISBN: 978-1-4759-5685-6 (ebk)

Library of Congress Control Number: 2012920221

Printed in the United States of America

iUniverse rev. date: 12/04/2012

TABLE OF CONTENTS

LEGAL DISCLAIMER

A lawyer's job is to create a better strategy than the one you have, or the one that you just have not yet thought of. My Firm's strategy in every case is to evaluate the law and the facts, and design a conscious and deliberate process specifically for you. It is our belief that our process will ensure future success in your case.

-Brian D. Perskin, Esq.

Anatomy of a Divorce

Hire a Lawyer

Hiring a lawyer for your divorce will help in speedy processing of the paperwork and negotiating issues like child custody, finances, and property division.

File a Summons For Divorce

You must file a summons to start your case, which contains the basis for filing the divorce in writing, and notifies your spouse that a divorce has been commenced. Prior to filing, you must buy an index number from your County Clerk's office.

Serve Your Spouse with a Copy of the Summons for Divorce

The defendant (your spouse) must be served with a summons and s/he must receive it personally. If the defendant cannot be located, alternate service for delivery may be used after getting permission from the court where the divorce was filed.

Wait at Least 20 Days for Your Spouse to File an Answer

After serving the summons, the defendant has 20 days in which to file an Answer in court.

File a Request for Judicial Intervention

A Request for Judicial Intervention (RJI)* must be filed no later than 45 days from service of the summons.

An RJI must be filed no later than 120 days from service of the summons if a Notice of No Necessity* is filed by both parties.

*See Glossary for further description.

Statement of Net Worth

A Statement of Net Worth must be exchanged and filed no later than 10 days prior to the preliminary conference.

Preliminary Conference

A preliminary conference must be held within 45 days of the RJI filing date. **NOTE:** Both parties must be present, and the judge shall address the parties.

Discovery

Discovery shall be completed and a Note of Issue filed no longer than 6 months from the date of the Preliminary Conference, unless otherwise ordered by the court. This includes the exchange of the all bank accounts, credit card information, Pension Appraisal Reports, Interrogatories, and Examinations Before Trial (commonly known as Depositions).

Compliance Conference

Compliance with the Preliminary Conference is assessed at a conference, unless the court dispenses with it based upon a stipulation of compliance filed by the parties. **NOTE:** Parties must be present unless otherwise advised by the court.

Pre-Trial Conference

At the Pre-trial Conference, updated Statements of Net Worth as well as Statements of Proposed Dispositionsand Witness Lists must be filed with the court.

Trial

A trial must be scheduled no later than one year from the date of the Preliminary Conference.

Please refer to NYCRR § 202.16(f) for further information.

Introduction

A divorce is one of the most stressful events that you may encounter in your lifetime. This book will provide you with precise, detailed, and exact directions on how to create a winning divorce strategy by guiding you through various tactics that I have garnered from my 22 years of experience as a divorce attorney in New York City. These tactics are designed to ensure that you are in the best possible position throughout the case, from filing for divorce through trial.

My years of experience working with clients of all backgrounds have taught me that being upfront and speaking the truth will save you time and avoid unmet expectations. Through this experience, I have trained an extensive staff of attorneys and paralegals in the ways to best assist you in your divorce. This book will demonstrate in detail, and through numerous examples, the divorce secrets that we have discovered, and that my team now applies, that have helped countless clients who are going through the same process you are now likely enduring.

My firm and I are familiar with the mistakes that individuals who are considering initiating a divorce, or those who are entrenched in litigation, make; this book will help you avoid those pitfalls. I will reveal the knowledge and experience we have garnered from actual cases, which can save you thousands of dollars and hours of time. Experience is not something you can just download from a free website, or even learn in law school. Instead, these tips have been obtained from real-life cases and from watching countless attorneys repeat the same errors. Without a game plan in place from the outset, you are setting yourself up to lose and face potential humiliation in court. Even further, you will endure a long and emotional litigation process and possible financial ruin.

Take control of your divorce now. You will not regret the decision.

CHAPTER 1

Winning Divorce Strategies

Crafting a Winning Divorce Strategy

When clients come into our office, they are all essentially asking us what they should do. Every day, my team and I speak with all different types of people about what to do in their particular case, and day in and day out, we encounter the same mistakes made by individuals and other attorneys that are easily avoidable had they been more familiar with the court system. Unfortunately, a divorce is akin to a war; one does not go to battle without being sufficiently prepared and without considering every strategy prior to engagement. This book will detail the tactics we have learned and the mistakes that we have seen that you will wish to avoid with the goal of maximizing your happiness and ensuring that you achieve the best possible outcome.

The Essentials of a Personalized Winning Divorce Strategy from the First Meeting

Anyone who contacts my office is told that he or she must first meet with one of our attorneys for a consultation in person. Unlike other lawyers, we firmly believe in a lengthy introductory meeting, wherein you as the client will detail the status of your case and how we can help you. Speaking and listening to each person provides us with the information we need to devise a strategy specific to each

1

client. This meeting is not a sales pitch; instead, it serves as a vehicle for us to learn about you and the means by which we may help you. If you choose to hire our firm, this meeting is essential to guaranteeing that your case is on its proper course. In certain instances, this may mean working toward a settlement through a formal offer, while other situations may require the filing of a suit in court to safeguard that person's best interests. The initial consultation is therefore essential and requires a client who is upfront and open to discuss strategy.

In deciding which lawyer to hire, pay attention to the questions that are asked during your initial consultation, and make sure that at that initial meeting you are getting advice. When clients come into our office, we first need to get a basic overview of the case. We need to know: names, ages of the parties, ages of the children, employment history, a list of assets – both separate and marital, the parties' present living situation, the general demeanor and attitudes of their spouse, and a general schedule of the children's routine, including who primarily does homework with the children, who attends doctor appointments, and who attends parent-teacher conferences. We also need to know if there is a history of violence, including confrontations in front of the children, and who controls the family's finances. Once we have this information, our next question is always: "What do you want?"

You should only choose a lawyer who is willing to litigate to achieve the results that you want. If a client tells us what s/he ultimately hopes to achieve and we determine this unreasonable, we politely apologize and inform that individual that our firm cannot be of assistance.

Where the Case Will Go After the First Meeting

Almost any competent lawyer can figure out how to file divorce papers in New York, but a divorce lawyer is more than a paper pusher. A divorce lawyer is your counselor and your chief strategist. Strategy is not taught in law school and can only be developed over a long career and through proper training; your divorce lawyer should not only be familiar with how to file the necessary paperwork and the proper relief to request in a New York Court, but should also be able to strategize the perfect time to file for divorce or the right motion to apply for seeking immediate relief. Your divorce lawyer should look at both the short- and long-term strategies.

A week does not go by where we are not amazed at the ignorance of certain attorneys who blindly give out advice or file suit without any hint of strategy or any knowledge of the facts of that client's case. These lawyers either file for divorce in cases where their client should clearly have waited, or they ask for relief from the Court that has little to do with the actual situation the parties face. What many divorce lawyers do not understand is that the court system is an ever-evolving one; for example, the way that papers were filed several years ago is completely different today. Every individual who is going through a divorce needs a lawyer who regularly practices and shows up to court in front of the same judges. This ensures that you have a lawyer who is up-to-date with the current legal procedures, court processes, and the different personalities of judges that may preside over your case.

Do not choose a lawyer that simply tells you what you want to hear. Choose a lawyer who has the courage to tell you the truth about your case, even if the truth is contrary to what you wanted or expected to hear. Once you hear the truth about the actual law applied to the facts of your case, and not a sugar-coated version of what might happen in a perfect world, you can make the best decision for you and your family. Do not think about your case as winning or losing; instead, think about how to best achieve your goals, given your specific set of facts. Every case is different, and hiring a lawyer that treats every case the same will lead to your dissatisfaction with the outcome of your case. If you want general advice that is given to everyone without any examination of the facts of your case, you can receive free generic information on the court system's website.

Be Prepared to Litigate or
Waste Your Money Negotiating

After our initial meeting, there are a number of avenues that you may pursue. It is essential to remember that every case has a beginning, middle, and end. If appropriate to the circumstances, we will urge clients to immediately file for divorce, thereby putting pressure on your spouse to either settle or litigate.

Generally, my team and I are willing to attempt to settle for 30 days before involving the courts. If this fails, we will often file suit. Delaying your case through endless negotiation with your spouse will only cost you money and will lead to little progress. Too much time is wasted by lawyers trying to negotiate a settlement out of court. If settlement cannot be accomplished within 30 days, forget about it. While both you and your spouse may want to settle, without a judge acting as the referee, most lawyers simply tell clients what they want to hear. Consequently, the case goes nowhere. Our experience has shown us that cases settle quicker if the Court becomes involved.

Familiarity with the court system is therefore essential in crafting a highly efficient divorce strategy, which may then be tailored to the particular judge who is assigned to your case. For example, the assigned judge may be particularly unsympathetic towards fathers with regard to the matter of custody, thereby requiring a strategy that changes the conversation to decision-making and access. On the other hand, some judges may favor fathers, allowing your strategy to focus more on the mother's negative attributes to build your case. Familiarity with the judges in each county is essential.

Following the filing of the initial paperwork with the Court and the service of process of these documents, your case will be scheduled for a Preliminary Conference, which serves as an introductory vehicle between the Court and the litigants and establishes a roadmap by which your divorce will proceed. Prior to the Preliminary Conference, a Statement of Net Worth must be prepared, listing your assets, expenses, liabilities, and income and requires the production of your tax returns, W-2 forms, and 1099 forms. At the Preliminary Conference, the Court will determine what has been resolved and the remaining outstanding issues and will then set up a timeline by which the exchange of financial documentation will occur.

Judges commonly tell you how they think they are going to rule almost from the outset, including giving a speech at the first appearance stating how much time and money this will cost you and who is going to have primary custody of the children. Do not be put-off: this is done to scare you in an effort to force you to settle. At this point, the judge does not have all of the facts, evidence, and information available; the only time a judge has all of the facts is after a trial. It is always essential to follow the strategy set by your attorney from the initial stages to the final trial if necessary.

Ultimately, if your matter is not resolved, you will appear for compliance conferences and a pre-trial conference until the Court eventually schedules your case for trial.

The Importance of Having a Lawyer Who is Prepared to go to Court

It is crucial to engage the services of a divorce attorney that is not afraid to litigate in court. This is an absolute MUST as the courtroom is a critical bargaining venue. If you have a lawyer that is unprepared to appear before a judge, you maintain little bargaining power. Even further, a lawyer must be prepared to stand up to a judge and fight back to protect your best interests. If you wanted a "yes-man," you could appear without representation; acquiescing to a judge's demands or those of your spouse's lawyer does not require a law degree.

The Power of Knowing the Other Side

Aside from an overall strategy and familiarity with the court system, your lawyer must have a good understanding of opposing counsel and any other individuals that may be associated with your case, including an attorney for your children or any forensic evaluators. A lawyer who knows all of the other players will be well-informed and will be able to factor their roles into your overall plan.

Given what is at stake, an ambush by opposing counsel with a tactic that you were completely unprepared for is unacceptable. Therefore, your strategy will also depend on your spouse's attorney and your spouse. Knowing who the other party is that you are opposing will determine the rules of engagement and the foundation of your winning divorce strategy.

Be Prepared

As stated at the outset of this book, your divorce must be treated seriously and often presents itself as a zero-sum game: if you are unprepared and have not crafted a strategy that best protects your interests, you will likely suffer. This book is designed to assist you through various tactics and through real-life examples my team and I have encountered to best ensure that you are successful personally and financially.

Chapter 2

Divorce Considerations

A ll relationships may be considered turbulent and emotional at times, but if you are consistently having more downs than ups, you may be looking at divorce as an appealing option. If you are unable to get the idea of filing for divorce out of your head, you need to truly think about the consequences of this decision.

How to Tell Your Spouse

You will probably not blindside your spouse with the news that you want a divorce, unless he or she has not been paying attention to your recent problems. For this reason, we advise potential clients to hire a divorce attorney before telling your spouse; being the first to file may provide you with an advantage.

Your Spouse's Response

It is impossible to know how someone will respond to the news of divorce. An angry or surprised spouse may react in one or more of the following ways:

- Complete silence
- A request for an explanation
- A quick exit to go think alone
- Various threats

If your spouse reacts with a threat, it will often involve money or your children. For example, your spouse might swear that you will never get maintenance or any of your shared assets. After 22 years of practicing law, I have trained my team to know how to continue moving the case forward so that your spouse's threats do not work. The uncooperative spouse could even get into legal trouble for using stall tactics, so rest assured that this approach will not work for him or her.

If you have kids, your spouse will likely threaten that you will never see them, even if you are currently the primary caregiver. Fortunately, your spouse would be wrong in most cases. Most courts frown on parents using their kids to gain an advantage, and this type of threat will likely reduce your spouse's chances of obtaining custody. Most judges want to help both parents to be involved in their children's lives, which means that as long as you can provide a safe, loving home for your child, you still have a chance for custody.

Are You Afraid to Leave Your Spouse?

If your partner has made you afraid to get a divorce, it is important to let your attorney know before you inform your spouse of your decision. We have helped many terrified spouses escape a dangerous environment. Your attorney can help you obtain an Order of Protection to ensure your safety and that of your children.

Get Help Notifying Others of Your Divorce

One of the most difficult aspects of the divorce process is figuring out how to inform others. If you are worried about how friends and family members will react, remember that they will likely support you in your time of need.

If you are not sure how to tell everyone, know that you are advised to notify others in a way that seems fitting. When it comes to your best friends and family members, a phone call or in-person chat might be the most personal approach. Once you are ready to let others know, you might consider easier, faster ways, such as through text messages and status updates on social media sites. However, do not make any written or publicly derogatory comments about your spouse.

Telling Your Kids

Telling your children is likely what you may dread most. If you have been delaying, realize that having your kids find out from other people is far more damaging than any approach you might take. As major decisions are being made, such as one parent moving out, you need to let your kids know as soon as possible. Letting them be blindsided when their mother or father moves out is not advisable.

Many couples choose to have a family meeting to discuss divorce. If you choose this approach, you and your spouse should schedule a date and time to gather your kids into one room at home. Make sure you have their full attention as you announce the divorce, and keep in mind how they are feeling. Let them know they may ask anything they need to in order to better understand what is happening. However, this approach is not advisable if you and your spouse are unable to be together without bickering or blaming.

Some children handle the news better than others. But be aware that even if your children seem like they are fine, they may begin struggling in school or while socializing. Many children are not great at communicating their feelings, so their negative emotions may manifest in other ways. Be sure to closely observe your kids long after the divorce process has started.

If it seems your children are coping well, it may be because they understand the benefits of the divorce; just like you, they may feel relieved that their parents can finally end the constant arguments. Since the divorce rate is unfortunately so high, they probably have several friends whose parents are divorced, which can help them process the news.

Stay on the Same Page as Your Spouse

You and your spouse may not be able to agree on much, but you most likely both love your children and want to make sure they are okay throughout the process. This is why you should generally speak with your spouse before telling the children about the divorce.

Be sure to avoid blaming your spouse, and do not speak badly about the other parent. Make sure your spouse understands this, too. If you can agree on just one thing, this should be it.

CHAPTER 3

The Divorce Process

B efore you decide whether to proceed with a divorce, you first need to learn the main steps you will have to take. You will not be divorced in one day, or even within a few months after you officially commence the court case. The process takes time and necessitates significant thought before making any official decision.

The following are common steps that most divorcing couples in New York will go through:

- Filing for Divorce and Service of the Papers
- Temporary Orders
- Discovery
- Settlement or Trial

How to File and Serve the Papers

Residency Requirements in New York

Prior to filing for divorce in New York, you need to ensure you meet certain requirements. For instance, if both you and your spouse live in New York, and you've lived here for a certain period of time, and the reason for your divorce occurred here, then you meet the requirements. Or, if you were married here and one of you still lives in this state, the residency requirement is only 1 year. The same goes if the grounds for divorce arose in this state, or you both lived in New York together and one of you still lives here.

Filing for Divorce and Service of Papers

Once you know you meet all the requirements[1], you may institute an action for divorce in one of two ways. First, you may file a Summons with Notice that simply and briefly states what you are asking for. Second, you may file a Summons and Complaint that contains detailed information as to what you seek. Either way, the document must state the grounds for divorce, the current residence of both you and your spouse, and the day and location where you were married. If you have children together, you will also need to list their names and birthdates.

A process server will deliver the documents to your spouse, who will then have to answer and appear in the case. Your spouse will eventually need to state whether he or she agrees to the complaint, which will determine whether you will have a contested or uncontested divorce.

Temporary Orders

A divorce frequently takes months or even years to complete, but your life does not stop during that time. This means you still need to deal with child support and alimony, and some simple rules need to be established and followed by both you and your spouse in the beginning of the proceedings. This is where temporary orders come in to play.

Temporary orders can direct child custody, child support, alimony, and payment of the bills on the marital residence. When children are involved, the main goal of temporary orders is to ensure that the children have a stable home during the divorce. Most judges do not like to add additional changes to the lives of the children, so they are likely to keep the kids with the current

---

[1]   For further discussion on the requirements, see Appendix A.

primary caretaker. The children may not end up staying with that individual permanently, but until the divorce has been finalized, they will likely stay put. If our client is the spouse who is granted temporary custody of the children, we also file for temporary child support. Otherwise, our client may not see the money s/he deserves for a long time.

Any temporary orders issued are in no way permanent, but do not underestimate the power they have in getting the final outcome you desire. Your best bet is to start out with the results you want so that it is more likely that the judge will simply leave the orders in place. You can do this by being the first to file court papers, which means speaking with a lawyer before your spouse does. Although temporary orders may be reversed at a later time, the first orders issued are often strongly considered by the judge, particularly if they appear to be working.

At times, the temporary order is far greater than the final order because of the judge's lack of knowledge about the particulars of the case. When an attorney goes into court and asks for upfront relief for their client, the judge's most immediate concern is making sure that the spouse with no money is taken care of during the interim of the proceedings. In many of these situations, the judge is merely making a "guesstimate" based on the limited facts provided.

Benefits of Temporary Orders

There are several benefits to obtaining a temporary order. Particularly, when a good temporary order is issued by a judge at the beginning of the proceedings, we quite often see no reason to rush the case, especially if our client is the non-monied spouse. Temporary orders can be used as key leverage in final settlement talks. Since in many cases the temporary order is far greater than the final order that will be issued, there is no immediate need or reason to want to settle. You can drag the case out over a long period without having the need to settle because you are receiving solid financial support.

If you are the spouse without the money, it is always a better strategy to threaten to drag the case on, which will incur higher fees and thus will create leverage for the other party to settle. A divorce is a process of negotiation, and the last thing that the monied spouse wants is to be hit with large legal fees. Knowing that your spouse is sensitive to high legal fees will give you the leverage that you need to create a quick and beneficial settlement. This is why you need a lawyer that is not afraid to create turmoil and put pressure on the spouse with the money so that s/he is willing to settle.

Discovery

Once the papers are properly served and signed, the discovery process begins, which involves getting accurate financial information from your spouse, typically through the help of several documents. Keep in mind that the more documents that can be produced, the better the chances of impressing the judge, who just wants to see each spouse comply. As long as the client makes an effort to help the discovery process go quickly, the judge should see that person in a favorable light during the case. In every divorce case there is mandatory financial disclosure.

What Documents Will Be Requested?
Most judges require the production of the following documents:

- Pay stubs for current and past jobs
- Evidence of any stock options, bonuses, or retirement benefits for current and past positions
- Personal tax returns
- Business tax returns for any owned businesses
- Checks written in recent years
- Credit card statements
- Bank statements
- Proof of real estate bought and sold both before and during the marriage
- Life insurance policies
- Health insurance information

- Value of certain personal assets, including antiques and family heirlooms
- Values of all vehicles
- List of monthly expenses
- Mental and physical health records
- Marital and non-marital debts

You must make every effort to get the required documents. Anything that cannot be obtained needs to be explained carefully to the judge so that it is obvious that every effort was made to comply.

It is important that you have a lawyer who is familiar with analyzing discovery produced by both parties. In my 22 years of experience, I have found that most spouses attempt to hide or distort certain details. There may be discrepancies involving the value of the home or business: one may either overestimate or underestimate the numbers in an attempt to profit, while others may claim to make less than he or she actually does in order to reduce spousal support or child support payments.

Analyzing the documents your spouse has provided and extrapolating general patterns can greatly affect how your case proceeds. Discovery is an important component of any divorce case since the results have such a profound effect on the case.

Settle or Go to Trial

After the process of discovery has been completed, you must decide whether you believe you can resolve your issues outside of the courtroom; if not you and your spouse will ultimately go to trial. In deciding whether or not to go to trial, be sure to consider both what the judge has said and what your lawyer recommends based on the particular details of your case.

Settlement

In the event both parties agree to settle, both will have to sign a Stipulation of Settlement that states which assets each person will receive, and which responsibilities, such as debts, each is assigned. If there are children, the agreement will state who gets custody, and it will also discuss child support, visitation rights when applicable, and any other outstanding issues. The Stipulation will then be filed in court.

Trial

If the parties are not able to agree outside of court, plan on going to trial. Remember that you, your spouse, or both of you, could lose in the courtroom, and there is no way to know the outcome ahead of time.

Keep in mind that the judge who will make the ultimate determination does not know you or your spouse well. In the end, this person will decide on important details that will seriously affect your life, either in a good or bad way. The judge does not truly know which parent is best for your children, and he or she does not really know which person deserves the house, retirement funds, or other assets. When you go to court, this person will be left in charge of these decisions, and the outcome could end poorly. This is the risk you take when you go to trial.

CHAPTER 4

Recognizing the Opposition

There are three broad types of lawyers who represent divorce litigants: The Settlor, The Negotiator, and The Bully. Identifying and recognizing which type of lawyer is on the other side will help you formulate a strategy that will benefit you and help you come closer to reaching the resolution that you seek.

The Settlor

A majority of the lawyers who take divorce cases are either inexperienced, too busy to actually analyze the facts, or actually do not specialize in divorce and family law. Most of the time, these lawyers want to settle the case immediately, either because they cannot identify the real issues in the case, they fear they will not get paid, or, quite frankly, they really do not care about doing the best possible job for their client.

In our practice, once we have identified our opponent as a Settlor, we immediately take charge of the negotiations, and urge our clients to make settlement offers that include the best possible outcome that they are seeking. For example, if our client is the spouse with the greater financial resources, and holds a greater share of the assets, we offer very little money and explain to our adversary how his/her client will receive even less at trial. On the other hand, if we represent the spouse without the assets, and we recognize the other lawyer as a Settlor, we immediately demand the sun, the moon, and the stars. We explain to the Settlor that we will not stop because that is what our client will achieve in court, thereby scaring that lawyer and the opposing client about the amount of work and legal fees to come.

The Settlor simply wants the case over and is likely to recommend these types of settlements to their client, even if it is not the best outcome. The Settlor is generally apathetic towards the actual results of the case and is more interested in just closing out the file, without any regard to the client's overall welfare. This type of lawyer will be overmatched by an experienced practitioner, and if s/he does not concede to almost every demand, s/he will likely come close.

The Negotiator

Many lawyers, even experienced ones, want to negotiate every last aspect of a divorce settlement. Although we recognize such a need to negotiate, sometimes negotiations take on a life of their own. Lawyers who tend to over-negotiate are generally scared to actually go to court. Once we have recognized an Over-Negotiator, we push the case forward to seek judicial intervention. Since the goal of any divorcing client is to settle their case quickly and efficiently, moving your case before the Court will actually save you money in the long run.

The Bully

Many lawyers can manage a lawyer that is either a Settlor or a Negotiator, but few attorneys know how, or have the capacity, to defend a client against a Bully. The Bully lawyers are easy to spot: they are loud, obnoxious, file multiple motions with the Court, make unreasonable demands in meetings, and will do or say anything to get you to either give up, or completely settle on their terms.

The first rule of dealing with a Bully is to not back down; fight fire with fire. If the other attorney wants to attempt to intimidate me by filing needless multiple motions, we will file our own set of motions asking the Court to prevent such abuse. In every one of my motions where we believe that the other lawyer is just trying to intimidate my client into settling, we will ask for legal fees so that our client does not suffer financially.

It is important that the lawyer you hire to deal with a Bully has a fully functioning office, with associates and paralegals that can assist with defending against a Bully. Bully lawyers have a habit of filing motions and writing letters on Friday afternoons, or when your primary lawyer is on vacation. This is not done by accident. Every action taken by a Bully is done purposefully and with the intent of getting the other to give up and settle on favorable terms.

Bully lawyers will say or do anything to win. If you hire the wrong lawyer who is either not experienced or equipped to deal with this type of opponent, the results could be disastrous. Although many lawyers are afraid to challenge a Bully, we are not easily intimidated. For years, clients have been hiring our firm based on our experience, intelligence, and ability to stand up for our clients. My office's primary concern is getting the best result possible.

No matter who represents your spouse, my staff and I will fight, argue, and protect your legal rights to the best of our abilities. This business is about results for our clients, not about making friends with the opposition.

CHAPTER 5

Winning Custody Strategies

C ustody and access are often the most contentious and emotional issues families encounter in splitting apart. Preliminarily, in deciding custody, courts will look to the past to determine who has primarily acted as the caretaker for the children. Judges ultimately seek to ensure that the best interests of the children are being promoted in settling the final custody and access arrangement. Therefore, it is of utmost importance that you act in a manner that puts you in the best light; whenever you are fighting for custody or access to your child or against access of another to your child, you should always begin by saying that you want as much time as possible. Remember, a judge may be considering your actions in the near future.

Approaching Custody Arrangements

It is always best to be the one to initiate the custody "conversation" and be the first to put your case forward for wanting the children to live with you (or whatever schedule you are asking for). Clients generally present two overarching scenarios: 1) they have acted as the primary caretaker in the past, or 2) they have been involved in the children's lives but did not have final decision-making. No matter the situation, we emphasize how critical it is to continue to assert your role in the children's lives, while also communicating with your spouse.

The Importance of Evidence

If you intend to obtain custody of your children, you must have the evidence to demonstrate that either you are the parent who is most fit for parenting or that your former spouse is not competent. Of course, you can also decide to do both, but no matter what, you must have the evidence to support your claims. Typically, this strategy works best when you are the primary caregiver, thereby increasing your ability to prove that your efforts have ended in positive results.

Gather Evidence That Shows Your Parental Fitness
In order to demonstrate that you are the more-fit parent, there is often an abundance of evidence at your fingertips. For example, if you claim that you regularly take your children to the doctor when necessary, you should gather all medical records and bills, which prove that your children get the regular medical treatment they need. Similarly, if your claim is that the children do well in school when living with you, it is helpful to obtain their report cards and comments from their teachers. If you want to show that you have a room set up for your children, you should take pictures of the bedroom, showing that your kids have their own safe place to stay when they live with you.

Anything that shows your children are succeeding under your care can help your case. Simply telling the judge that you are the right custodial parent for your kids will not convince him or her. You need proof, and fortunately, it is usually easy to get.

Gather Evidence That Your Former Spouse Is Not a Fit Parent
There is also documentary evidence you can gather to demonstrate the other parent's unfitness. For example, if you know your ex gets into a lot of trouble with the law, you should get copies of any police reports that show he or she was arrested. The same goes if there have been any accusations of child abuse. If your children often have bruises and broken bones after staying with your ex, take pictures and gather any medical records or school paperwork that

documents the injuries. These documents can go a long way toward keeping your children with you, not your former spouse.

The Importance of Keeping a Log

While progressively building your child custody case, it is crucial to maintain a log of any events that happen when the children are under the care of your spouse and yourself. The log should include information such as:

- interactions you have with the child
- interactions you have with your spouse or the child's other parent
- every pick-up and drop-off
- what you did with the child while in your custody
- what the child ate
- when you gave your child a bath, depending on the age of the child
- any injuries in your care or spouse's
- anything else of any significance

All of these events may be used to show that you are responsible and willing to foster and maintain a relationship between yourself, the child, and the other parent.

Write down *everything* that occurs during your interactions with your children. Often, it is helpful to take contemporaneous notes. The reason for this is because someday your custody case may go to trial, and it is really difficult to remember what someone did or said a year or more before. When you testify at trial, it is like you are painting a picture and you want to make it colorful. Having a record will make your testimony more colorful, as it will help you to remember specific occurrences. If you do not write things down, you risk putting yourself at a major disadvantage.

Information is the key, and the more detailed the information is, the better off you will be. If you do not keep a written record, all you are able to say is, "I want custody of my kids," and without any supporting evidence, your case will be weak. In fact, if you are asked what you did a year ago with your child and you cannot remember, you will be put in a terrible position at a trial.

Crucial Point
Never Discuss Money and Custody at the Same Time

Whenever you are fighting for custody or access to your children, *never bring up money in the same conversation.* It is imperative that you segregate the discussions about custody and finances, including child support; they must be separate topics. The issues of custody and access to children are a completely different conversation to the amount of child support payments that should be allocated.

The two topics should never overlap or merge, nor should one topic be used as leverage for the other—i.e., a parent offering to pay more money in order to have more or less visitation rights. Judges, therapists, and forensic examiners will come down against you for merging these issues during negotiations. This puts you in a very bad position and is the worst thing to ever say. Anything to do with kids, or kids seeing their parents, and parents making decisions about their children, is a completely different conversation than how much child support is going to be paid, *or how much equitable distribution is going to be given.* **NEVER hire a lawyer that merges those two conversations.**

Strategies for Progressive Rights to Custody

When we represent a non-custodial parent, we tell him/her to look at the custody issue as a progression. We begin by asking what the custodial parent is willing to allow regarding access, and then proceed accordingly. For example, for the first week, access may be as little as one hour, but then this gradually builds up to several hours in the following week, and more time after that, as it is proved to the other party and the judge that the non-custodial parent is a responsible and accountable caregiver that can be trusted with the child. The plan is therefore progressive, and over time we can begin to ask for longer visits, moving to short overnight visits and gradually progressing to whole weekends.

In situations where young children are involved, it is generally beneficial to drag the case out, because it gives the non-custodial parent the opportunity to demonstrate to the Court, or the hearing examiner, that s/he is a responsible caregiver, and the Court will feel comfortable in letting him/her have greater access, and eventually custody, of the child. This will only help as the child ages.

Advice for Fathers

Fathers facing divorce are often anxious that it will reduce their time with their children. Although your spouse may threaten that you will never see the children after the divorce, this is rarely the truth. Furthermore, it is not proper to use the children as pawns during this process. Just because your partner does not understand this, does not mean that you have to stoop to the same level. Instead you must act proactively but within the letter of the law to protect your rights as a father. If you want sole or joint custody of your children, you maintain the same right to litigate as the mother does.

A typical case that we are presented with is a mother with a young child who does not want the father to have overnight visits and is nervous about the father having access to the child for extended periods of time. These mothers often argue that the father does not know how to bathe the child, diaper the child, feed the child, etc. Situations like these make the custody process a long haul, although simple complaints, like the father does not know how to use a car seat or how to put the child to sleep, can easily be overcome.

Generally when a mother comes to me with this type of approach to custody, I explain very clearly that every father has a right to see their child, and I **will not** take on cases where mothers refuse to allow fathers access. There are small exceptions to this rule: where there is physical abuse, emotional abuse, a history of drug abuse, or there is anything that can put the child in danger.

Attorney for the Child – What You Need to Know

Under the Family Court Act, all children in divorce or custody cases are appointed a lawyer to help protect their interests and to allow them to express their wishes to the Court. The attorney for the child is an advocate for the child and is not a guardian *ad litem*. A guardian *ad litem*, or "GAL", is appointed to protect the interests of a person under a legal disability, not to advocate the child's position. A GAL has a responsibility of exploring the truth on the issues and recommending a resolution to the Court. On the other hand, barring certain severe instances, the attorney for the children will not substitute his or her judgment, and will only advocate what the child wants.

An attorney for the child has an obligation to consult with the child and advise the child to act in a manner that is consistent with the child's ability to understand the advice being given, and the attorney for the child should have a thorough knowledge of the child's circumstances. The wishes of the child should be paramount in shaping how the lawyer for the child advocates for his client. When a child is capable of understanding and stating his/her position, the attorney for the child must be guided by the wishes of the child. The attorney for the child has the obligation to fully explain all the available options to the child and may recommend or suggest the best course of action to the child that would promote the child's best interests.

An attorney for the child is ethically bound to represent the client's wishes, even if the attorney has an opinion that is in direct opposition to the child's. Absent very limited circumstances, the attorney must advocate based upon the client's wishes. A child client is entitled to independent and effective representation, which is only accomplished by the attorney having regular contact to ascertain the child's wishes and concerns and to counsel the child regarding the proceedings. However, courts have ruled that when an attorney for the child is either convinced that the child either lacks the capacity for understanding their wishes, or if the attorney for the child believes that the child may be in a substantial risk of imminent and/or serious harm, the attorney for the children would be justified in advocating a position that is contrary to the child's wishes.

Selection of the Child's Attorney

For custody disputes litigated in Family Court, an attorney for the child is assigned by the Court, often from organizations such as The Children's Law Center. This is done at no cost to the parties. Conversely, in actions litigated in Supreme Court, the judge will ask the lawyers to agree on the selection of an attorney for the child, and the parties are responsible for paying that attorney. It is important that your lawyer has input into the selection of the child's attorney. Although there are clear and concise rules regarding the conduct and representation provided by the attorney for the child, many of them come with their own set of biases and beliefs. Since every custody case has its own unique set of circumstances, it would be beneficial to select an attorney for your child that would best suit the facts of your particular case. In many instances, an attorney for the child is instrumental in assisting the parties to come to a fair resolution. The selection of an experienced and fair attorney for your children can save time and money in resolving your case.

Overall, the matters of custody and access must be treated with care and in an intelligent manner, spanning prior to filing though the end of trial.

CHAPTER 6

Engaging the Services of Professionals in Custody Cases

I n divorce and family law cases, the services of professionals are generally engaged in two ways: one will be for custody matters, and the other will be for financial issues.

Forensic Examinations in Custody Matters

For custody issues, courts often appoint a forensic examiner to do psychological workups of all the parties involved, including all the caregivers (parents, grandparents, and significant others) and the children, to aid the judge in making the best custody decision.

Judges generally give the lawyers the option to select the forensic expert. An experienced divorce attorney who is well-connected and knows the other players in the game can select the right expert for your case. Even though there has to be agreement on both sides, some attorneys just let the client pick the forensic examiner. This is lazy work.

We pick forensic experts that may be favorable to my client depending on the case. For instance, some forensic examiners are more favorable to men, while others favor the mother. It is imperative that your lawyer knows which examiner to use for your particular circumstances. Having this insider knowledge may be the key ingredient to a winning divorce strategy, as the opinion of the examiner can really sway the case one way or the other.

Working with Forensic Examiners – Preparation is the Key
A crucial component of your interaction with forensic examiners is to ensure that you are well prepared for what to say to the examiner. Answering certain questions correctly will be a major determining factor as to who will get custody or access to the child, hence the high importance placed on careful preparation before the examination takes place. Many clients simply have no idea what to say or how to answer questions properly. Through my years of experience, my team and I have learned certain tips for interacting with examiners.

First, we ensure that our clients are well prepared to answer the anticipated questions of the examiner. My office has a list of questions that we run through with each of our clients, and we always remind clients that the examination is NOT about bad mouthing the other parent – in fact, this is quite often frowned upon and will likely not get you the result that you want.

Here are some of the basic questions that we use to prepare our clients for forensic examinations by psychologists:

- What are your parenting methods?
- What are the particular needs of the child?
- How does the other party's parenting method meet or neglect the needs of the child?
- How well do you cooperate with the other parent to address the child's needs?
- How are you able to support the other parent's relationship with the child?
- What is your current living situation and how does that benefit the child?
- In what ways can you demonstrate that you make appropriate decisions for the child?
- Are there any of the following behaviors or factors apparent in the other parent: alcohol or substance abuse, interference with access, sexual or physical abuse, or alienation by the parent?

Positioning Yourself as the Most Suitable Caregiver

Your goal in a forensic examination is to explain to the examiner why you are the better parent. However, the reason behind why one party is better than another does not necessarily have to do with how *bad* the other is.

Be careful not to play the angle of trying to demonize the other party – that is not what the examiner is looking for, nor should it serve as your strategy. Examiners view those that bash the other spouse as dramatic, insincere, and as the type of person who has a tendency to blame and lack senses of clarity.

It is better to focus on yourself: what makes *you* a great parent. The examiners are more interested in the facts and evidence about what it is that *you* do for the child and why you are better suited to be the custodial parent. Your winning edge and your leverage is to explain, with evidence, why you are the better parent, why you would be the best person to take care of this child. Go into the examination with this approach: "I think I am better for these reasons and this is what I do."

Generally, the only times that it is necessary to broach negative information about the other parent is if that person is a physical danger to your child, in the event of significant abuse, or alcoholism. In those situations, the best interests of the children are at risk, and it would be careless not to bring that information to the examiner. However, that information should have been shared with a judge well before a forensic examiner was appointed.

Furthermore, you need to be organized when you enter the meeting with the examiner. Anger-fueled accusations or unprepared answers without facts and evidence will be detrimental to the assessment. For example, if you are the parent that attends all of the parent-teacher conferences and you also share that information with your spouse, then you will be deemed to be the responsible parent that is highly accountable and can be trusted to have custody of the children. Similarly, if your child is having an issue with other children at school, you should be sharing that information with your spouse – and keeping the evidence of doing so through an email. The reasoning behind this is that judges and forensic examiners look at which parent is better at fostering a relationship with the other.

The forensic examination is about presenting yourself in the best possible light that shows why you are the better person that should be in charge of the children. You need to be seen as cooperative and a good communicator that is not only good at taking care of the child, but also at sharing information with the other parent and fostering a relationship between yourself and the other parent.

TIP: *No matter how crazy the other spouse is, this is not about them, it is about YOU. You need to present yourself in the best possible light and take the focus off the other parent. Your sole purpose in a forensic examination is to explain why you are the fit custodial parent, better equipped to make decisions for your child.*

CHAPTER 7

Winning Financial Strategies

W hen dealing with the financial elements of a divorce, a well-planned financial strategy process is crucial. The following elements are the basis for this strategic process:

1. Plan: Gather financial records and develop financial plans for the near future and long-term;
2. Research: Assemble a complete list of assets, income, expenses, and debts;
3. Strategize: Understand the short-term and long-term impacts of divorce settlement offers; and
4. Review: Assess settlement proposals.

Planning: Getting a Clear Roadmap to Your Financial Future
When clients come to us looking to begin divorce proceedings, it is important that they have a clear roadmap of their financial future. This means critically thinking about how you are going to continue to support yourself and your children, as well as envisioning various roadblocks along the way.

In many situations, a divorce puts a roadblock in people's financial plans. Quite often, one party has no idea how to take care of the simplest financial activities, such as paying bills and writing checks, much less the more complicated activities like managing brokerage accounts. They also have little or no understanding about matters such as whether to sell a vacation property, the consequences of remaining in the marital residence versus moving out, and generally planning out their post-divorce financial roadmap.

Researching: Taking Your Financial Inventory
When visiting your lawyer, you should prepare by getting your finances in order and taking your financial inventory. This is the beginning of the pre-planning of your post-divorce financial landscape.

You should be sure to have access to, as well as detailed knowledge of, documentation regarding:

- The assets in the marriage
- The purchase date of the assets
- The income of each spouse
- The debts that exist within the marriage

Having this information ready to present to your lawyer will ensure that you have taken stock of your life, and thus know what you are dealing with. It is impossible to move forward and create a winning financial divorce plan if there is insufficient information about the current state of your financial affairs.

A divorce is much like a business deal – before you sell a business, you need to take stock and value each item appropriately in order to determine the true worth of each asset.

Asset Splitting

Many lawyers do not understand the concept of each case being different and are quite satisfied with splitting everything 50-50, right down the middle. **But 50-50 does not necessarily always mean what you think it means!**

Assets have different values that depend on a number of factors, which must be taken into account when negotiating the divorce settlement. A *winning* divorce strategy recognizes that splitting everything down the middle can often be disastrous and not a true reflection of the worth of the assets. This is where your lawyer needs to be able to guide you and explain the nuances in the true valuation of assets and to calculate any potential increase or decrease of your total net worth.

Retirement Accounts

Retirement accounts in a divorce proceeding can be divided in several different ways, including by means of a Qualified Domestic Relations Order (QDRO) or by simply presenting a judgment of divorce which orders a division of individual retirement accounts.

Retirement accounts can also be traded: the value of the retirement account is exchanged for actual other property in the marriage. When trading a retirement account for other property, one party can decide they want the entire pension, so the pension is valued and traded off against the equity in another asset.

Asset Hiding

It should come as no surprise that people attempt to hide money and other assets from their spouses. When asset splitting, you may not be aware that your spouse has a large sum of money hidden in a secret account. I have seen far too many people over the last 22 years who were married to someone who hides money. Asset hiding can occur in two different ways:

The First Type of Asset-Hiding Group

The first type of asset-hiding group are people who are in cash businesses and do not report their income to the government. Here it may be difficult to trace exactly where the money and assets are hidden due to several reasons, including:

- The cash is not placed in a bank account
- Credit cards are not used
- Transactions are cash based

However, one can prove income by reverse engineering the process to prove what the spouse actually spends. For instance, if your spouse argues that s/he earns little money but s/he is driving an expensive car and has a high mortgage or rental expenses, you can use these expenses as evidence that s/he is in fact generating more income than what is actually reported. The Court may then impute income to that individual. This is why it is essential to have a clear and detailed financial inventory and record of the household expenses to utilize as evidence.

In certain cases, you may need to perform some degree of financial discovery to obtain copies of documents, such as the application for the financing of a car, mortgage request, or credit card applications to strengthen your case in proving that there is asset or income hiding taking place. The most efficient way to obtain copies of these documents is through a subpoena. While lawyers generally know how to subpoena documents, it is crucial to hire a lawyer that actually knows what specific questions to ask and what particulars seek.

The Second Type of Asset-Hiding Group

This second group includes people who earn significant money but have multiple bank accounts, make numerous transfers, and fail to disclose all of the bank accounts that belong to them. In these situations, you must trace the money at the point of receipt. For example, if your spouse works for a firm on Wall Street and the money comes in to one bank account, then your job is to follow where that money goes after the initial deposit.

Quite often in divorce cases, individuals with significant wealth either intentionally or unintentionally omit certain accounts on their statement of net worth. So it is our job as your attorneys to investigate and obtain a clear, detailed, and complete financial picture of the spouse. When cases become overly complicated, we often hire an experienced forensic accountant to go through a detailed analysis of all the records to assist us in the process of tracking the money.

Conducting Business Audits

In many cases, your spouse may be hiding money and assets within his/her corporation, and an audit of the business records is helpful in determining unexplained accounts, balances, or transfers. These investigations may become extremely complex, and your lawyer must have a solid understanding of financial matters and the ability to peruse bank statements and other financial statements clearly.

The Importance of Having a Divorce Lawyer to Guide You toward a Solid Financial Future

The true goal of any divorce strategy is to settle as quickly and effectively as possible. This is why it is crucial to hire an attorney with a strong financial background, investigative skills, and experience with similar cases. However, only upon having a complete picture of your family's finances will you be able to make a determination about how to best achieve your goals.

Once you have provided your lawyer with the full scope of information required, your lawyer can then tell you, based on his or her experience, what a particular judge may rule given your personal circumstances, such as the age of the spouses, your incomes, and ages of the children. While this is certainly not an exact science, if you hire a practitioner that does this on a daily basis, you are much more likely to receive a reasonable estimate of what to expect in your particular case.

An experienced attorney will be able to determine what you can reasonably expect, and once you are comfortable with the future projection, your aim is to ask for more, thereby adding a buffer to allow you to settle comfortably after negotiation. On the other hand, if we are representing the more financially secure spouse, we will offer less than that estimate.

The bottom line is that your lawyer should have a sound understanding of financial matters, as this is crucial to the final outcome and will have serious consequences regarding your future.

Tax Implications of Divorce

Most lawyers do not have any understanding of the tax implications in a divorce. **As a result, you may wind up walking away from potentially thousands of dollars of tax deductions simply because your lawyer did not have the requisite experience and knowledge.** A planned, smart, and well thought-out tax strategy is the cornerstone of any divorce settlement.

Tax Free Exemptions

It is important to know the tax consequences related to certain transfers of property, assets, and other financial instruments as they may potentially be transferred tax free. As an example, in the case of the sale of a marital home, a single person can receive approximately $250,000 in the form of a tax free exemption. In some cases, it might make sense to take the marital residence and let your spouse receive the securities that will be tax impacted.

Child support is always tax free, whereas alimony or maintenance may be either taxable or tax free. If there is nothing stated in the divorce agreement, the default assumption is that it is taxable to the person receiving it, and tax deductible to the person paying it. In situations such as these, high income earners benefit from paying more in the form of alimony as opposed to child support. It is a win-win situation for both parties.

Handling Debts in a Divorce

It is vital to have a clear picture and documentary evidence of all of the marital debts, including those in existence and those that have yet to be incurred, because they are also marital property that must be divided appropriately.

Every Case is Different!

Each divorce case is different and is comprised of different facts and circumstances. The final outcome is dependent on the particular case: the facts, the evidence, and the judge that is hearing the case. This knowledge can put you in a winning position from the outset.

CHAPTER 8

Forensic Examination in Financial Matters

When a Business Evaluator is appointed to a case, the purpose is to evaluate a person's professional license or degree, corporation, partnership, and/or real estate interests. It is critical to retain a lawyer that not only agrees that a valuation needs to take place, but that can also understand the report.

Business and Asset Valuation in Divorce Cases

Any lawyer you hire should not only be able to understand financial reports, but should be knowledgeable enough to question the data and figures reported, as well as the actual expert who produced the report.

The initial report must be closely examined, and, due to the numerous variables, your lawyer should have familiarity with how utilizing different metrics will affect the valuation of the particular asset. Often, this requires using different scenarios that can significantly impact the values. "Goodwill" in the valuation of a business is a perfect example.

When experts value a business, they add the estimated goodwill of that business, which is a vague and subjective term. Goodwill is an intangible asset and is usually described as the difference between the sales price of a company and the value of its tangible assets. Goodwill is based on the company's reputation, customer loyalty, competitive advantage, and even high employee morale. Therefore, when an expert says the goodwill of your firm is one million dollars, you need to really inquire as to whether that is an accurate and relevant number.

Understanding and Dissecting Business Valuation Reports

Far too often, the parties involved in a divorce – including the spouses, attorneys, judges, and even the business owners themselves - lack the unique background to thoroughly understand business and asset valuations. While the hiring of business valuation experts is highly beneficial, the reports themselves are often complicated, loaded with industry jargon, and difficult for the ordinary person to comprehend.

In valuation, experts must understand accounting numbers and also need to be highly skilled at developing financial projections, thereby restating the accounting figures so that the economic and financial reality of the current business and economic climates are considered. In many cases, business valuation reports focus on "accounting" numbers, which look backwards, reflecting history, while "valuation," when performed correctly, must be forward-looking. The economic climate can change rapidly, and the past is not always a valid reference point for determining the future value of a business.

A credible business valuation must take into account the following:

- The general state of the economy
- The state of the specific market in which the business operates
- Competitors
- Interest rates
- Company specific opportunities
- Company specific risks
- Ownership structure

These factors are by no means an all-inclusive list. There are numerous other factors that my firm is highly experienced at detecting and questioning. In my practice, my staff and I make sure that we question all of these numbers, and bring to light the significant factors that impact your business and future projections.

We have encountered numerous lawyers who examine a report and simply accept it on face value, trusting that what the experts say must be true. Clearly, this is not the best way to handle these reports. It is necessary to understand that just because an expert publishes a report, it does not mean that that its results are correct and that it should not be further investigated using different variables. Most lawyers do not know this and will not even attempt to question the figures that are presented, which can lead to disastrous outcomes.

The impact of the evaluator's report may be colossal, the difference between zero to millions of dollars. Just like each divorce case is different, so too is the business valuation report. Consequently, the report must be examined based on the individual facts and circumstances. These slight differences can have a significant impact on the value.

CHAPTER 9

Winning Maintenance Strategies

I n New York, the term "alimony" is not used; instead New York courts will award "maintenance", which is money that one may be required to pay to the other spouse during or after a divorce.

Maintenance Issues –
People Can Only Pay What They Can Afford

When making maintenance demands, you must remember that people can only pay what they can afford. There is little point in asking for money that you will never receive.

While the husband or wife with access to money may be ordered to pay a certain amount of maintenance per month, if this is not enough to meet the needs of the other, it will be necessary for the spouse receiving maintenance to consider supplementing his/her income by finding work. The spouse with the money is not expected to support the other indefinitely. Judges in New York State will look unfavorably upon a lawyer who claims that their client can make zero dollars. Zero is not an option

Lawyers must counsel their clients about how to obtain employment and what judges will expect from them in the form of contributions towards taking care of themselves and their children.

Pendente Lite Maintenance

Pendente lite maintenance is maintenance that the judge will award for the pendency of the action, for either a court-ordered amount of time or until a final decision is made and the case concludes. The purpose of *pendente lite* maintenance is to keep each spouse in the lifestyle that they were accustomed to during the marriage, and is determined based upon the parties' respective incomes.

In 2010, New York State enacted a temporary maintenance statute to dictate the applicable, or "presumptive," amount of *pendente lite* maintenance using a formula based upon the parties' respective incomes. While courts are bound to follow this formula, it is my experience that an increasing amount of judges are reticent to apply it. Instead, judges often alter the presumptive amount of maintenance on the basis that the award is "unjust or inappropriate." Other judges simply delay an award of *pendente lite* maintenance in an effort to encourage the parties to settle the case. However, at the present time, the statute is law, and judges are bound to apply it.

In your request for *pendente lite* maintenance, it is important to convey your side of the story to the judge. You should include details of your marriage in a way that persuades the judge to look upon you favorably. Remember, you never get a second chance at a first impression. It is important to hire a lawyer who can present a request that is detailed, well written, and, most importantly, well reasoned. A knowledgeable lawyer will know that it is acceptable to stretch a little, but do not ask for things that are ridiculous. Over the last twenty years, I have read motions drafted by other lawyers that are poorly written and make little sense, and oftentimes their clients suffered as a result.

It is equally important to hire a lawyer who can best defend your case should your spouse file his/her own well written and well reasoned motion. Your affidavit in response will become part of the court file and could be used against you down the road. Do not swear to something that is not true. A lawyer who does not take great time and care in preparing your response will have disastrous consequences for you. If a judge perceives you as untruthful with regard to one aspect of your case, how would you expect the judge to trust you in the remainder of the case?

Determining the Right Amount of Maintenance

Judges in New York do not generally award large amounts for maintenance; they give an amount which is considered justified and fair to both parties. Maintenance should never be considered as an invitation not to work for the rest of your life simply because your ex-spouse is a high-income earner.

It is important to remember that there is only so much that you can get from one person and one paycheck. It is far too common for lawyers to not be transparent on this issue and to allow their clients to accrue massive legal fees.

Length of Maintenance is Dependent on the Length of the Marriage

Both short- and long-term arrangements for maintenance should be considered. Quite often, maintenance payments will be high in the short term, but they are eventually reduced over the long term. The amount is determined based on a number of considerations, including the length of the marriage and the amount of child support being paid.

Generally, maintenance lasts for about half the time that the couple was married, with a decreasing rate of payment. So if a couple was married for 12-13 years, the maintenance entitlement will generally be for 5-7 years, at a decreasing rate.

We always tell our clients that there may be some short-term pain in terms of maintenance payments, but this will only be in the initial period.

CHAPTER 10

Negotiating a Win-Win Settlement

The goal in any divorce case should be to reach a settlement agreement. Likewise, in a child custody dispute, reaching a custody and/or visitation agreement will save you money and time. To reach a fair settlement agreement, it is necessary for both parties to bargain and negotiate. Cultivating strong negotiation skills will aid you in resolving your current dispute and with any issues that may arise in the future.

The purpose of a negotiation is problem-solving by creating an acceptable solution for both parties. While there are no set-in-stone rules for negotiating, there are a few techniques and considerations to keep in mind when meeting at the bargaining table:

- Prepare a strategy of what you want;
- Put aside your emotions;
- Have respect for all parties; and
- Be willing to compromise.

Assess and Strategize

Before meeting to negotiate your divorce or custody agreement, it is a good idea to sit down with your attorney to determine your priorities. First, what are you least willing to give up? Second, what are you most willing to give up? Third, what are the things you believe the other party would be least/most willing to give up? Be sure to look at the entire picture of your marriage and determine what it is that you value most.

You should plan some concession points: those things that you are willing to give up in order to get something that you really want. You must also be able to back up your position, so it is important that you are prepared to answer questions that clarify your position. You will need to be able to say, "I want this because . . ."

Choosing the Right Lawyer

Be sure that you choose a lawyer who you work well with. In the 22 years that I have worked as an attorney, I have met all different types of clients, and I have trained my staff to ensure that they listen to what our client wants in order to achieve his/her primary goals. Not every lawyer does this, though. You want a lawyer who is going to represent your interests above their own.

You must also be aware of, and plan for, coercive tactics that the other party (or lawyer) may utilize, including lying, hiding facts, personal attacks, threats, playing on your sense of dependency, belittlement, unreasonable demands, and refusing to even negotiate. If any of these tactics are used against you, it is important to have an attorney who can recognize them for what they are and who has extensive experience in responding to them.

Always Move Forward

The only topics open for negotiation are those that have not been previously decided. Returning to past issues that were already decided may have the effect of causing the agreement as a whole to fall apart, leaving you back at square one. Once you've agreed on something, check it off and move on.

Remain Calm and Control Your Emotions

When negotiating, it is easy to get sidetracked and dissuaded by heightened emotions. Negotiating takes a lot of energy and often will bring to the surface old hurts and resentments. The process can be incredibly frustrating, and if you allow these feelings to take over, you will never reach a satisfactory agreement.

Allowing feelings of pride, anger, or manipulation to enter in while trying to negotiate will only lead to escalated conflict. Do not be confrontational or taunt your spouse. Remain focused on the goals of the negotiation, the problems at hand, and let go of the blame.

Avoid Retaliation

Even if the other person becomes irritable, taunting, or even cruel, responding or retaliating is not helpful. Even though it may be incredibly difficult, you need to remain calm. Judges want parties to settle. Even if you cannot reach an agreement, at the very least you will be viewed as the one who is actively participating in the settlement process.

If either you or your spouse becomes too emotional at any point during the negotiations, a cool-down period should be taken. It is best to discuss this with your attorney during your strategy session: when you begin to feel uncomfortable, you should have a way to signal that you need to take a break.

Keep in mind that the point of the negotiations is to come to a win-win agreement. The best way to do this is to remain calm.

Respecting Your Adversary

Knowing what you want and what you're willing to give up is the easy part. Learning to show respect for a person you may have been extremely hurt by, or that you are incredibly angry at, is more difficult. When you show respect to your adversary, negotiations are more likely to move forward.

Once a respectful atmosphere is in place, it will be easier for both parties to understand and identify with each other's positions, thereby making a resolution more likely. Here are some tips for acting respectfully:

- Do not be rude, confrontational, or insulting.
- Do not be defensive and try not to take things personally. Try to be open to constructive criticism.
- Try not to escalate a negative situation. For instance, if the other person insults you, do not be quick to retaliate. Simply ignore the put-down and focus on getting to an agreement.
- Do not refuse to negotiate or give ultimatums. Try to keep an open mind about the issues. If there are things you want more than others, use the things you do not want as bargaining tools.
- Listen carefully and quietly, and do not interrupt. At the same time, make sure that when it is your turn to speak, the other person and attorneys present give you the same courtesy.
- You do not need to be friendly, but you should try to be polite.

Willingness to Compromise

Probably the most important element to effective negotiations is the *willingness* to compromise. Compromising embodies all of the elements discussed previously: strategy, emotion, and respect.

Bargaining with the knowledge that you are going to have to compromise on certain issues actually gives you a one-up on your adversary. When you say no to what your adversary wants, you can suggest another solution that is more in-line with what you desire. What are you willing to trade for what you really want?

Compromise but Do Not Yield to Pressure

Be careful not to be forced into a decision. Never agree to something when you are feeling pressure from your spouse or your attorney. The agreement that you are negotiating will not be up for further discussion once signed, so it is imperative that you are comfortable with each element included. If you are uncomfortable with what is being said, voice your concern and explain what it is that you do not like.

Final Tips for a Successful Negotiation

When you begin to negotiate, remember to focus on your end goals: get what you want, sign an agreement, and move on to your future. To do that effectively and with as little agony as possible, here are some things you should remember:

- Strategize – what are you willing to give up and what aren't you willing to give up?
- Be respectful of your adversary; be polite.
- Listen attentively and do not interrupt.
- Be willing to compromise to get those things that you really want.

CHAPTER 11

Divorce Tactics to Watch For

Be Careful Who You Trust –
Attorney Tactics to Watch For

W hen it comes to divorce, you should hire a lawyer who you can trust implicitly, and who knows how the opposing lawyer operates and practices. Many lawyers are not trustworthy, and it is always advisable to obtain everything in writing. Documentation is essential; people are likely to lie, particularly regarding issues regarding their finances.

Avoid Relying on Your Emotions to
Run Your Divorce Strategy

My office has seen numerous cases where clients instruct their lawyers to file multiple motions with the Court, as tedious and irrational as it may be, simply to aggravate their ex-spouse. We will not act in such a manner, we will never jeopardize clients' cases, and how they are perceived by the Court, by pandering to them, especially when they are being irrational. We are very clear with clients about this. Our sole purpose and aim is to provide the most solid, well-planned, and strategic legal advice. Our purpose is not to make friends; clients do not hire an attorney to act as a "yes-man".

Some examples of inappropriate filings are motions on who should walk the children to school, who should feed the children breakfast in the morning, whether pick-up time should be 6:00 or 6:30pm, or whether vacation time should decrease from eight days to six. Motions such as these are a waste of everyone's time and money.

Your Lawyer is Not Your Therapist

The emotional issues associated with a divorce are often some of the most difficult that the divorcing parties face. Because people are emotionally attached to each other, they let their emotions affect the way that they think. This is why you need an experienced and clear-minded lawyer to set you straight and guide your decision-making.

However, it is important to remember that your lawyer is not your therapist, and you need to deal with your emotional issues separately. There are far too many clients who want to talk to their lawyer numerous times a day, and there are even more lawyers who will allow this, while letting the client pay the huge legal bills that result.

We always make sure that our clients are aware that we are not therapists. We will always take the time to listen to what our clients have to say and take their needs into account, but we make it clear that if they are experiencing emotional and psychological issues, that they should consult a therapist. A therapist is cheaper and is more experienced in dealing with the psychological and emotional effects of a marriage breakdown. We are here to get the job of your divorce done – which means a winning divorce strategy that will benefit you for years to come, long after the emotions have worn off.

Our goal is to give you the best legal advice and to guide you through the legalities of the divorce process in the most effective way possible. In the end, clients should care most about meeting their goals. The last thing that you want is a lawyer that is going to play with your emotions and fight simply for the sake of fighting.

Alienation of One Parent

Alienation of One Parent by the Child

In our experience, actual alienation of one parent is quite rare. According to New York State law, actual alienation of a parent occurs when the child refuses to speak to or see a parent. People throw around the term "parental alienation syndrome" quite often, but from the evidence that I have seen, this is an overused term and does not accurately reflect what is happening in a particular situation between a parent and a child.

Under the New York System, parental alienation is taken seriously if it reaches the point where the child in question refuses to see one of the parents. Ex-spouses may be difficult and annoying and might make it hard for one parent to see the child, but this is not the level at which it would constitute parental alienation. The child must actually not want to see or speak to the parent.

While it may be easy to prove that your child does not want to see you or speak to you, the difficulty is in demonstrating that this is the fault of the other parent. A more effective strategy is to simply prevent it from happening in the first place. To do so, we advise parents to be aggressive and fight for as much time with their children as possible while maintaining constant contact with the children.

Alienation of One Parent by the Other Parent

Alienation by a parent occurs when there are attempts made by one spouse to alienate the other parent by influencing the child. However, this does not constitute parental alienation under New York State Law; a mere feeling of alienation is not sufficient. It is the rare case that a New York judge would actually find parental alienation.

When a client asserts that the other parent is alienating them, the first question we always ask is when they last saw or spoke to the child. Quite often, the client will tell us that it has been a year or more. If this is the case, it is usually the fault of that parent for not being proactive and making sure that they have regular and consistent access to their children. If you do not reach out to your child, or if you do not go to court asking for more access, it may not necessarily be the other parent's fault. Parents must also put in the effort to ensure that they have regular visitation with their child.

It is easier to prove that actual parental alienation has occurred when there is a court order for a parent to have visits and the other parent has impeded the access as set forth in that order.

CHAPTER 12

Winning Strategies That Are Not Talked About

Behavior towards Your Spouse during the Course of the Litigation

Communication with Your Spouse

It is important that you act in a professional and calculating manner towards your spouse prior to and during the divorce proceedings. Every form of communication between you and your spouse may be used in court as evidence. Make sure that the record of your communications, created using emails and text messages, strengthens, not harms, your position in court.

Important Note: *Do not under any circumstances send any derogatory or angry emails, text messages, or voicemails to your spouse, his/ her family, or his/her friends.* Your emails should be used only to convey factual information, without any commentary. In New York, divorce lawyers are famous for attaching emails and copies of text messages to court papers and quoting from the same in court. An angry or derogatory message may even result in your spouse receiving an order of protection, which may have a ***major impact on all aspects of your case.***

Important Advice on Written Communication
Utilizing emails and text messages may aid you in achieving your objectives as it is easier to create a record using written communication than it is with telephone calls. For example, if one spouse wishes to have extended time with the children, s/he should immediately start creating a record through emails of his/her requests for access. The emails should include:

- Requests for more time with the children
- Asking for a calendar of the children's activities
- Inquiring when the next parent-teacher conference will be held
- Finding out the time and place of doctor appointments
- Requesting contact information for the children's teachers and doctors
- Asking for the names and addresses of the children's friends
- Telling your spouse that you want to arrange play dates for the children
- Calling your children's friends' parents to arrange play dates or weekend excursions

It is imperative to not just ask but actually follow through on your inquiries.

Judges are primarily concerned with what is happening in the children's lives now and *how important a role you play in them.* Judges could not care less that you worked twenty-four hours a day two years ago or you never attended a parent teacher conference for whatever excuse. An up-to-date written communication record is hard evidence of the importance of your presence in your children's lives.

Another situation in which written communication is invaluable is if you feel that your spouse is spending too much money prior to the commencement of the case in court. Use email correspondence to inform him/her that you are unable to afford such a lavish lifestyle. If you choose to cut back on some of the extras that you have enjoyed over the years, you must make sure to keep your spouse informed through emails. Additionally, you can create a budget that shows the dramatic cut-back in expenses, and then communicate this budget to your spouse via email.

Be clear and concise in all your correspondences, and do not put anything in them that may portray you as untruthful. *A well thought out and balanced campaign will best serve your interests in a divorce proceeding.*

Orders of Protection

Most spouses tend to use orders of protection as a sword rather than a shield. If your spouse is able to obtain an order of protection, you can be removed from your home against your will, and your spouse may be granted temporary exclusive use and occupancy of your home. Additionally, the first time you call to speak with your children or are ten minutes late for a visit, your spouse will be on the phone with either the police or his/her lawyer. This will result in another motion being filed, casting you in further negative light before the judge, and costing you more money.

The Importance of Image –
How to Act during the Case and In Court

There are a certain mistakes that poorly-advised litigants consistently make in their divorce proceedings. Some important rules of thumb to keep in mind include:

- Never speak to the opposing lawyer without your lawyer's presence and permission
- Never "cc" the opposing lawyer in emails. All communication should come from your lawyer directly.
- Never show any emotion or attitude to your opposition.
- Do not disclose the witnesses you may call if your case proceeds to trial until necessary
- Do not speak or react when on the record before the judge.

Controlling Your Emotions

It is important that the opposition should have as little information about you as possible. If you are a nervous person, or tend to get angry quickly, there is no reason for the other lawyer to observe these traits. Inevitably, if you show emotion in the hallway of the courthouse, the opposition will use these against you before the judge.

You should not speak to your attorney within earshot of the opposing lawyer. While it is natural for you to be emotional and show your true emotions, the opposition may see your reaction as a weakness, and the attorney may then counsel your spouse not to settle, knowing you would be a terrible witness at trial. *Never give the opposing counsel any insight into what type of witness you would be.* If you act appropriately in court, you provide the opposition with as little information as possible.

Your Role at All Court Proceedings is to Sit and Observe

Never under any circumstances speak directly to the judge while on the record, unless the judge asks you a direct question. Never interrupt your attorney, opposing counsel, or the judge. You can and should take notes and discuss these points with your lawyer either quietly if the judge gives you time in the courtroom or outside the presence of your spouse and his/her lawyer.

Arguments before the Judge

For the most part, court appearances are status conferences, allowing the judge to monitor your case, to ensure that discovery is progressing, and to check that settlement negotiations are ongoing. Unless a specific motion is on the calendar, there is no reason for either lawyer to make arguments before the judge.

The judge should only consider written motions and their responses. Many litigants, as well as lawyers, get sucked into arguing points in open court that are not pending before the judge. A good judge will dismiss the argument and tell the lawyer to file a motion to be heard. Any response should include a general denial and an explanation to the judge that, when a proper motion is filed before the Court, your client will file responsive papers that will outline his/her position.

Taking Care with the Use of Modern Technology

Social media websites, such as Facebook and Twitter, contain a bounty of personal information. These websites have become effective tools for attorneys who are looking to procure personal information on their clients' spouses.[2]

Divorce lawyers can easily access Facebook pages using websites like Flowtown.com, which allow users to enter an email address and subsequently view various social media profiles or individuals for hire to send a friend request. Mutual friends of the spouses are also a valuable resource. Most often, while the couple is going through a divorce, they de-friend each other, but they forget about their mutual friends. These shared friends "can play detective" and obtain otherwise confidential information from either spouse's profile. Once attorneys gain access to a profile, they will scroll through wall posts and personal information.

The number of divorce cases that utilize social media sites have increased exponentially over the last five years. In order to protect one's information, one must become familiar with the privacy settings. As a result of "social media stalking", divorce attorneys are able to poke holes in the credibility of their client's spouses. Information that an attorney retrieves from a social media website, whether it be uncovered affairs or the exhibition of unacceptable behavior online, may sway the outcome of the entire trial.

For those who use Facebook or other social media sites and are going to be involved in a divorce or custody battle, double check your profiles, edit them, tighten their privacy, be careful of what

---

[2]   *See* CNN.com, *Divorce Attorneys catching cheaters on Facebook*, June 1, 2010, *available at* http://articles.cnn.com/2010-06-01/ tech/facebook.divorce.lawyers_1_privacy-settings-social-media-facebook?_s=PM:TECH (last visited May 4, 2012).

you post, and take heed of Facebook friends who might not truly be known to you. Or, to undoubtedly ensure the protection of your personal information, it is easiest to temporarily deactivate your account.

Changing Passwords

Clients should also ensure that they change all of their passwords, including all email accounts, social media profiles, personal credit card accounts, and anything else that your spouse can access to use as evidence against you.

Conclusion

B
y now, you should be aware that you cannot enter into a divorce without knowing your options and without a clear plan. It is our hope that, by utilizing the strategies outlined in this book, you will avoid the mistakes highlighted to ensure that you are in the best position prior to the start of your divorce, during the case itself, and after the process is finalized. You must realize that a divorce is akin to a war; one does not go to battle without being sufficiently prepared and without considering every strategy prior to engagement. Speak to a lawyer, utilize the strategies presented herein, and act intelligently to protect your interests. You are now prepared to go forward; good luck!

APPENDIX A:

Common Divorce Questions and Answers

When beginning divorce proceedings, clients have countless questions, including what is involved, and how various aspects of a divorce are best handled. The following are the most common questions that I have been asked by those seeking a divorce.

What is a Divorce?

A divorce is a legal action between two individuals to terminate their marriage. It may be referred to as "dissolution of marriage," and it acts as the final termination of the union.

Where do I go for a divorce?

In New York, the Supreme Court and not the Family Court grants you a divorce. You are required to apply for a divorce in the county in which you live.

The Family Court is only able to assist you in matters pertaining to child custody, spousal maintenance, child support, and orders of protection.

What is an annulment?

An annulment establishes that a marriage is not legally valid. The difference between a divorce and an annulment is that an annulment finds that a union was never certified, while a divorce dissolves a valid union.

There are several ways to get an annulment, including proving one of the following:

- Bigamy: That one of the parties was still married to someone else at the time of the second marriage.

- That either spouse was incurably unable to have sexual intercourse at the time of the marriage.

- That after the marriage took place one of the parties became incurably insane for 5 or more years.

- That one of the parties is unable to comprehend the nature and consequences of a legal marriage due to a lack of mental capacity.

- That one of the parties entered into the marriage under duress or force exerted by the other party.

- That the marriage was fraudulent. This means that the consent to marry the other spouse was obtained through fraudulent methods that involved deception that was material enough to obtain the consent of the other party, who would ordinarily be a prudent individual.

Annulment is defined in Domestic Relations Law §140.

What are the legal requirements for a divorce?

(1) Residency: Before a New York court can grant you a divorce, one must show that you and/or your spouse have lived in New York State for a certain amount of time, without interruption, generally for one year.

(2) Grounds: You must have a legally acceptable reason to get divorced in New York. That means that you are required to prove one of the grounds listed below:

1) Cruel and inhuman treatment
2) Abandonment
3) Confinement in prison for 3 or more consecutive years
4) Adultery
5) Living separate and apart pursuant to a separation judgment or decree
6) Living separate and apart pursuant to a separation agreement
7) Irretrievable breakdown in the relationship for a period of at least 6 months (for divorce proceedings started on/after October 12, 2010)

Only the first 5 of these grounds require the finding of "fault," meaning some form of misconduct by one of the parties. If the parties have a separation agreement, the parties need simply to live apart for at least 12 months pursuant to said agreement. Both parties must sign and consent to the separation agreement.

"No fault" is the seventh ground for divorce, which does not require the finding of any type of misconduct by either spouse.

What is the difference between a contested and an uncontested divorce?

UNCONTESTED: Your divorce will be uncontested if both you and your spouse:

- Want to get a divorce, and
- Agree about what will happen with your children, your finances, and your property after the divorce.

CONTESTED: Your divorce will be contested if either you or your spouse:

- Do not want to get a divorce,
- Disagree about the grounds (legal reasons) for the divorce, and
- Disagree about what will happen with your children, your finances, or your property after the divorce.

Because the judge will require detailed information to decide the issues you disagree about, your contested divorce will require you and your spouse to go to the Supreme Court numerous times. If your divorce will be contested, you should consider finding a lawyer to represent your interest.

How do I begin divorce proceedings?

To begin your divorce, you first must buy an Index Number at the County Clerk's office and file either a Summons with Notice or a Summons and Verified Complaint. A directory of County Clerk's offices can be found in Appendix D.

You must ensure that your spouse is served with the Summons by a person who is over the age of 18 and who is not a party to the divorce action.

What if I am unable to locate my spouse?

New York State requires that the defendant in the divorce proceedings (your spouse) be personally served with the Summons with Notice or Summons and Verified Complaint. If you are unable to locate your spouse, you must obtain the permission of the Court in order to have them served in another way. You can apply for such permission by filing an application for alternate service with the Supreme Court Clerk.

Do I need to hire an attorney to get a divorce?

Due to the complicated nature of a divorce, it is always advisable to obtain the services of an attorney. You should do this even if you think that the divorce will be uncontested.

Do all divorces require going to court?

No, if you and your spouse agree on all issues, you may file an uncontested divorce that does not require appearing in court. However, these processes may not be appropriate in cases involving domestic violence or child abuse.

What types of matters can be dealt with in Family Court?

Although you cannot obtain a divorce in Family Court, Family Court judges hear cases involving child abuse and neglect (child protection), adoption, child custody and visitation, support, domestic violence, guardianship, juvenile delinquency, paternity, and persons in need of supervision (PINS).

What is a separation agreement?

A separation agreement is a written contract between spouses that divides all of the important aspects of the couple's lives: care and custody of children, money and property, and more. The spouses must then live separate and apart for a period of at least one year after signing a separation agreement in order for it to be used for a divorce.

What is a Preliminary Conference?

After you file a summons and a Request for Judicial Intervention, a preliminary conference will be scheduled where the Court will determine any possible issues that are in dispute. The point of the preliminary conference is to allow the judge to become acquainted with the case and the litigants. The judge will not make final decisions at the preliminary conference.

At the preliminary conference, the Court will impose strict guidelines for the production of financial documents and time frames in which to complete depositions. Also, if there are issues of custody/ and or access of the children, the Court will appoint a lawyer for the children. You may also discuss temporary orders at this time.

What is a temporary order?

Issues addressed in temporary orders include child support, custody, maintenance, or the marital residence at the preliminary conference. In general, any issues that need to be addressed immediately can be resolved in the short-term with temporary orders.

A temporary order is issued upon application to the Court. After a motion has been filed and briefed in full, each party will present the facts and argue the relief requested.

What is the Equitable Distribution Law?

When a court grants a divorce, marital property will be divided equitably (though not always equally) between the spouses. New York's Equitable Distribution Law divides property equitably according to certain rules, as opposed to common or "community" property states such as California where assets are divided equally (50/50 split). During a divorce, both parties are required to inform the Court and the other spouse about their income, their assets, and any debts they owe.

The Equitable Distribution Law distinguishes between two types of property for purposes of divorce:

> **Marital Property:** all property either spouse bought or earned during the marriage, regardless of whose name is on the property. Marital property includes, but is not limited to: cash, checking accounts, savings accounts, mortgages held, stocks, loans to others, business interests, cash surrender value of life insurance, vehicles, real estate, household furnishings, jewelry, art, antiques, precious metals, judgments, patents, pensions, 401Ks. degrees, and professional licenses. For certain assets, such as debts, pensions, degrees, and licenses, that were held prior to the marriage, the enhanced earning or debt on that property shall be considered marital, and will be divided by the Court.

> **Separate Property:** property a spouse owned before the marriage, as well as any inheritance, personal injury payments, or gifts from someone other than the spouse received during the marriage.

For a complete list of the factors a court should consider in making an equitable distribution award, see Domestic Relations Law § 236(B)(5)(d).

Is a credit check necessary?

Doing a credit check on your soon-to-be-former spouse will help to pinpoint exactly where their bank accounts are, what credit cards they have, and what other financial assets they maintain.

What about joint credit card accounts?

When dealing with joint credit cards, it is important to realize that most credit cards are not actually "joint," as they were originally opened up by one individual with the other simply being a second cardholder. The person who originally opened up the credit card is liable for any immediate charges.

It is a smart divorce strategy to make sure that the accounts on which you are the primary cardholder are paid off first, making it all the more crucial to take a thorough financial inventory as soon as possible. In this way, you can best avoid the negative consequences of a poor credit score.

TIP: Make sure that your divorce settlement agreement is designed to pay off your obligations first.

What should I do with debts that are in my name?

When you have a loan that was a part of the marriage but in your name alone, allocating the repayment of this loan to your former spouse can be disastrous. If your ex-spouse is late or fails to make the payments it is *your* credit rating that will be impacted.

What will happen to my business in a divorce?

Owning a business or professional practice can complicate the divorce process since it is a major asset that requires analysis. Whether you own a law firm, doctor's office, or other type of business, the value of the business must be determined, typically performed by a court-ordered neutral professional. In addition, you must determine whether the business is a marital asset that will be divided along with your other property or be treated as a source of income. If it is the latter, its profits will affect child support and alimony.

My spouse and I are co-owners of a business, now what?

If you and your spouse are co-owners or partners, dividing the business may prove difficult.

If the business is your only means of income or if it is significant to your family, you can continue to both own it. However, you will need to draw up the proper documents to make sure one spouse is not taken advantage of by the other in the future.

If the business model is too complicated to divide, you have the option of selling or splitting the profits fairly. If one of you wants to keep the business, you can arrange a buyout.

How is child custody determined?

When determining custody and visitation, a judge will prioritize the best interests of the children involved. Some factors a judge may consider include:

- Who has been the primary caretaker of the child
- Who the child is presently living with
- The home environment of each parent and how it will impact the child
- The determination by the judge of how fit they consider each parent to be
- The ability of each parent to provide emotional support
- How much involvement the custodial parent allows the non-custodial parent
- The choice of the child – if s/he is old enough

- Whether there would be separation from other siblings
- Whether any abuse has taken place

What is the difference
between legal custody and physical custody?

Legal custody is defined as having final major decision-making power for your child, including educational, religious, and medical decisions.

Physical custody refers to who the child lives with on a day-to-day basis. A parent with primary physical custody is sometimes called the "custodial parent" or the child's "primary caretaker."

Is there any preference of who is awarded custody?

No, there is absolutely no set-in-stone preference stating that either party should obtain custody. Both parents have the right to seek custody and visitation during a divorce. Domestic Relations Law section 240 states that there is no prima facie right to the custody of the child in either parent. The Court will consider the individual facts of each case when making custody decisions.

A parent who does not receive physical custody of the child will in almost every case be entitled to visitation rights.

What is child support?

New York law says that children are entitled to share in the income and standard of living of both parents. Child support is the money that the non-custodial parent pays to the custodial parent if the child is under 21 or otherwise emancipated. The determination of how much child support is generally paid is based on a formula.

Child support may be awarded by the Supreme Court as part of a divorce or in the Family Court as part of a child support proceeding.

How is child support calculated?

First, the Court determines each parent's net income. Net income is gross income minus certain deductions, such as FICA, NYC Income Tax, Yonkers Income Tax and spousal support. Second, the Court adds the parents' net incomes together and multiplies that number by a percentage, depending on how many children are of the marriage:

- 17% for one child
- 25% for two children
- 29% for three children
- 31% for four children
- No less than 35% for five or more children

That amount is then divided based on the proportion of each parent's net income to the combined parental net income.

In addition to the basic child support obligation, a spouse may also be required to pay for child care expenses, educational expenses, and medical expenses for the children.

Am I entitled to spousal maintenance (alimony)?

Spousal maintenance (sometimes called alimony) is money an ex-spouse may be required to pay the other spouse after the divorce is finalized or during the case itself. When spousal maintenance is ordered by the Court it is usually for a limited time.

If you are in the middle of a divorce, or still living together, you may be able to receive temporary spousal maintenance while the case is on-going.

What is *pendente lite* relief?

Pendente lite relief is awarded during the pendency of the action, for a judicially defined period of time, or until a final decision is made and the case concludes. In 2010, New York State enacted a temporary maintenance statute to dictate the applicable amount of *pendente lite* maintenance using a formula based upon the parties' respective incomes.

A well written application may ask the Court to make temporary decisions with respect to maintenance, child support, parental access, payment of household bills, and generally a continuation of the parties' present standard of living.

What is a penalty clause, and should I include it in the settlement agreement?

A penalty clause is a provision in an agreement stating that any late payment will incur a fee that is cumulative. This incentivizes your spouse to make timely repayments of the debt that is owed.

Because the court system and your lawyer often have very little control over what your ex-spouse does in terms of debt repayment, a simple and effective solution is to include a penalty clause in your divorce settlement to ensure that your debts are paid in a timely manner.

How do I obtain certified copies of divorce papers?

Copies of divorce judgments or other written orders in divorce cases may be obtained from the County Clerk. Copies of documents (other than the Judgment of Divorce itself) may only be obtained by one of the parties or an attorney who is representing one of the parties. Divorce records are not open to public inspection.

Can I modify the terms of my divorce after it has been finalized?

Yes, but only certain terms can be modified, including child support, child custody, visitation, or spousal support agreements. The occasional modification makes sense for most people since income, housing situations, and debts may change over the years.

If you wish to make these modifications, you will need to first prove that a substantial change has taken place. Common examples are that you have lost your job or income has been dramatically changed, meaning you are unable to continue paying the child support or alimony that you have been ordered to pay or the amount you are receiving is insufficient. You will need to furnish proof of this with an explanation as to why you are unable to continue operating under the current order.

If you can resolve these modifications with your former spouse outside of court, you are encouraged to do so. Many parents make amendments to the terms of child support, child custody, or the parenting plan. Changes will occur in both your life and that of your former spouse's life, so it is beneficial to both of you to be understanding. However, there are some modifications that your former spouse is unlikely to accept, and you might have to return to court.

Can my spouse or I file for bankruptcy during a divorce?

Either spouse can file for bankruptcy during the divorce. Regardless of whether the filing is joint or separate, assets of the marital estate – for example, the property acquired by either spouse during the marriage – may become part of the bankruptcy and are subject to liquidation to pay some or all of the debts.

When a bankruptcy filing is made in the middle of divorce proceedings, it will have the effect of slowing down and complicating the process. However, it may be essential and the best option for both parties.

Is it better to file for bankruptcy before the divorce proceedings begin?

Generally speaking, filing for bankruptcy before a divorce proceeding begins makes matters less complicated. This is not always practical or the most appropriate solution.

If it is determined that the best and most practical way to deal with the debts of the marriage is before the divorce proceedings commence, finalizing the bankruptcy before filing for a divorce will enable the couple to discharge a large portion of their debts. After the bankruptcy case is complete, New York courts will determine how to split the remaining debts and assets between the parties.

What happens if my ex-spouse files for bankruptcy after the completion of the divorce?

Some ex-spouses may decide to file for bankruptcy after the divorce in hopes of discharging some or all of the debts they were ordered to pay. Certain types of debts, however, are not dischargeable in either a Chapter 7 or Chapter 13 filing, including child support and alimony.

Can I protect myself if my ex-spouse files for bankruptcy after the divorce?

There are several ways for individuals to protect themselves in their property settlement agreements if they believe there is a possibility that their former spouse will file for bankruptcy after the divorce. These include:

- Indemnity agreements
- Property liens
- Support obligations
- Title changes on joint debts

Do I need a divorce lawyer with bankruptcy experience?

Divorce and bankruptcy can become complicated. If either you or your spouse is contemplating bankruptcy, it is crucial to hire a lawyer with experience in this area.

What is an automatic stay in a bankruptcy case?

Once a spouse files for bankruptcy, the Bankruptcy Court will issue an automatic stay, preventing creditors from continuing to attempt to collect any unpaid debts. The automatic stay also prevents the Divorce Court from proceeding any further with a few important exceptions.

The automatic stay does not apply to any actions to establish, modify, or collect support obligations, including spousal maintenance and child support, or to actions to determine paternity. In addition, the automatic stay does not apply to child custody or visitation decisions. In some cases, however, the automatic stay may make it difficult for a spouse to collect court-ordered support, particularly if the assets the other spouse would use to pay those obligations are considered part of the bankruptcy estate.

What do I do if I am the victim of domestic violence?

If you are the victim of domestic violence, visit your local court's domestic violence web page for information and resources. If you or your children are the victims of domestic violence, you can apply to the Court for an Order of Protection.

Where can I get more information?

Visit the Supreme and Family Court Web Sites. Even if you do not live in these counties, the web sites in Bronx, Kings, Nassau, New York, Queens, Richmond, Suffolk, and Westchester counties have helpful answers to Frequently Asked Questions and various forms.

Appendix B:

Income & Asset Analysis Checklist

Personal Benefit:	You		Spouse	
	Yes	*No*	*Yes*	*No*
401K Plan	☐	☐	☐	☐
Automobile Expense	☐	☐	☐	☐
Automobile Insurance	☐	☐	☐	☐
Child Care	☐	☐	☐	☐
Corporate Automobile	☐	☐	☐	☐
Corporate Credit Card	☐	☐	☐	☐
Dental Coverage	☐	☐	☐	☐
Disability Insurance	☐	☐	☐	☐
Education and Training	☐	☐	☐	☐
Employee Loan Policy	☐	☐	☐	☐
Eye-Care Coverage	☐	☐	☐	☐
Life Insurance	☐	☐	☐	☐
Medical Coverage	☐	☐	☐	☐
Profit-Share	☐	☐	☐	☐
Retirement Benefit	☐	☐	☐	☐
Stock Option	☐	☐	☐	☐
Vacation Benefit	☐	☐	☐	☐
Vacation Compensation	☐	☐	☐	☐

Other Assets:

	You		Spouse	
	Yes	No	Yes	No
Antiques	☐	☐	☐	☐
Art Work	☐	☐	☐	☐
Automobiles	☐	☐	☐	☐
Bonds	☐	☐	☐	☐
Broker Margin Account	☐	☐	☐	☐
Business Investment	☐	☐	☐	☐
Cash on Hand	☐	☐	☐	☐
Certificate of Deposits	☐	☐	☐	☐
Checking Accounts	☐	☐	☐	☐
Christmas Club	☐	☐	☐	☐
Coin Collection	☐	☐	☐	☐
Collectibles	☐	☐	☐	☐
Computers	☐	☐	☐	☐
Condominiums	☐	☐	☐	☐
Contingent Fees	☐	☐	☐	☐
Credit Card Reward Points	☐	☐	☐	☐
Credit Union Accounts	☐	☐	☐	☐
Deferred Commissions/ Benefits	☐	☐	☐	☐
Frequent Flyer Account	☐	☐	☐	☐
Gold/Silver Account	☐	☐	☐	☐
Gym Membership	☐	☐	☐	☐
Hidden Cash	☐	☐	☐	☐
Household Furnishing	☐	☐	☐	☐
Income Tax Refund	☐	☐	☐	☐
Inheritance	☐	☐	☐	☐
Intangibles	☐	☐	☐	☐
IRA Accounts	☐	☐	☐	☐
Jewelry	☐	☐	☐	☐
Keough Plans	☐	☐	☐	☐
Lawsuits (pending)	☐	☐	☐	☐
Legal Expenses	☐	☐	☐	☐
Life Insurance	☐	☐	☐	☐
Loans	☐	☐	☐	☐

Other Assets (cont'd):

	You		Spouse	
	Yes	No	Yes	No
Lottery Winnings	☐	☐	☐	☐
Money Market Accounts	☐	☐	☐	☐
Mortgage	☐	☐	☐	☐
Mutual Funds	☐	☐	☐	☐
Non-Existent Employees	☐	☐	☐	☐
Pension Plan	☐	☐	☐	☐
Profit Sharing Plan	☐	☐	☐	☐
Real Estate	☐	☐	☐	☐
Recreational Vehicles	☐	☐	☐	☐
Retirement Plan	☐	☐	☐	☐
Safety Deposit Box	☐	☐	☐	☐
Savings Account	☐	☐	☐	☐
Savings Plan	☐	☐	☐	☐
Scraps	☐	☐	☐	☐
Season Tickets	☐	☐	☐	☐
Securities	☐	☐	☐	☐
Severance Pay	☐	☐	☐	☐
Social Security Payments	☐	☐	☐	☐
Stamp Collection	☐	☐	☐	☐
Stock Options	☐	☐	☐	☐
Stocks	☐	☐	☐	☐
Tax-Deferred Annuity Plans	☐	☐	☐	☐
Tools	☐	☐	☐	☐
Trusts	☐	☐	☐	☐
Unreimbursed Business Expenses	☐	☐	☐	☐
Vacation Clubs/Units Vault	☐	☐	☐	☐
Workman's Compensation Award	☐	☐	☐	☐

Appendix C:

Glossary

Abandonment: Occurs when one spouse leaves the party for a continuous period of one year or more, without the party's consent, and without good cause

Access: See Visitation

Affidavit of Service: A signed sworn statement by a non-party who has served any papers, such as the Summons, in a lawsuit. The statement contains an oath that the papers were properly served

Alimony: See Spousal Maintenance

Annulment: An annulment establishes that a marriage that took place is not legally valid

Answer: Response to the Complaint

Asset Split: Division of the marital assets

Child Support: The money that the non-custodial parent pays to the custodial parent if the child is under 21 or not emancipated

Child Support Standards Act (CSSA): The Law that determines a party's child support obligation

Community Property: Assets are divided equally (50/50 split)

Complaint: A document containing the plaintiff's allegations of his or her reasons for a divorce

Compliance Conference: Court appearance to ensure that the discovery process has been completed to the satisfaction of both parties. An extension may be requested if discovery is not complete

Constructive Abandonment: Where one spouse has refused, without good cause, to have sexual relations with the party, continuously for a period of one year or more, without the party's consent

Contempt: One party's willful disregard or a court order. Contempt is usually punishable by fine, imprisonment, or both

Contested Divorce: Either spouse does not want a divorce, does not agree with the grounds for divorce, and/or disagrees agree about what will happen with the children, finances, and property after the divorce

Cruel and Inhuman Treatment: Consists of cruel treatment against the party that endangers the party's physical or mental well-being and makes cohabitation unsafe. Usually consists of physical, verbal, sexual, or emotional abuse

Custodial Parent: Parent with whom the children primarily reside

Custody: A parent's legal right to control his or her child's upbringing. There are two types: legal and physical

Default Judgment: Occurs when the Defendant fails to respond to either the Summons and Verified Complaint, or the Summons with Notice

Defendant: The person against whom the divorce or child custody action is brought.
Note: In an action for child custody or child support in Family Court, this person is called the **Respondent**

Deposition: Sworn testimony taken by an attorney in the presence of a court reporter. In New York a deposition is known as an **Examination Before Trial**

Discovery: Both parties provide documents regarding their finances, including assets and debts

Divorce: A divorce is a legal action between two people to terminate their marriage. It can also be referred to as dissolution of marriage.

Emancipation: The release of a child from the responsibility and control of a parent or guardian; usually the end of child support obligations. In New York, emancipation generally occurs at the age of 21, however, the child will also be emancipated if s/he marries or enters the military before the age of 21

Equitable Distribution: Property is divided equitably, although not necessarily *equally*, between the spouses according to certain rules

Estimated Goodwill: Intangible asset in business valuations; usually the difference between the sales price of a company and the value of its tangible assets

Examination Before Trial: See Deposition

Grounds: Legally acceptable reasons to get divorced in New York

Guardian *ad litem*: Person appointed to protect the interests of another person under a legal disability, such as age

Irretrievable Breakdown: Where the marriage is impossible to repair for a period of at least six months

Judgment of Divorce: Document signed by the Court granting the divorce

Legal Custody: The ability to make major decisions about the child, including: where the child goes to school, what kind of religious training a child receives, and medical decisions

Marital Property: All property either spouse acquired during the marriage, regardless of whose name is on the property

Monied Spouse: The higher-earning spouse

Non-Custodial Parent: Parent with whom the children do not reside

Note of Issue: Attorney's certification that all of the preliminary work on the case has concluded, and the case is now ready for trial. **Order of Protection:** Signed document by a judge that is filed against a family member or household member, prohibiting that individual from harassment, and in certain situations, ordering that person to stay away from another

Out-Of-Court-Processes: Include mediation or collaborative family law

Penalty Clause: a provision in the Divorce or Separation Agreement stating that any late payment will incur a fee that is cumulative, thereby incentivizing the payor to make timely repayments of the debt that is owed

Physical Custody: Who the child lives with on a day-to-day basis. A parent with primary physical custody is sometimes called the "custodial parent" or the child's "primary caretaker"

Plaintiff: The person who filed the divorce or child custody proceeding
Note: In an action for child custody or child support in Family Court, this person is called the **Petitioner**

Qualified Domestic Relations Order (QDRO): Establishes your ex-spouse's legal right to receive a designated percentage of your qualified plan account balance or benefit payments

Request for Judicial Intervention (RJI): A request for a judge to be assigned to the case

Residency Requirement: Requirement that you and/or your spouse have lived in New York State for a certain amount of time without interruption, generally for one year.

Separate Property: Property a spouse owned before the marriage, any inheritance or personal injury payments, or gifts from someone other than the spouse during the marriage

Separation Agreement: A written contract between a husband and wife that divides all the important aspects of the couple's lives: care and custody of children, money and property, etc.

Spousal Maintenance: Money an ex-spouse may be required to pay the other spouse after or during their divorce

Statement of Net Worth: A form required by the Court where you list all of your financial information in detail – income, expenses, assets, property and debts. It is a sworn statement that must be signed in front of a notary public before it is submitted.

Stipulation: A voluntary agreement between the parties on an issue or issues

Support: Payment to one spouse by the other for housing, food, clothing, and related living expenses

Temporary Order: A preliminary order issued by a judge that generally awards money for child support and maintenance.

Uncontested Divorce: Both spouses wish to get a divorce and agree about what will happen with the children, finances, and property after the divorce

Visitation: The right of the non-custodial parent to be with the child. Also commonly referred to as **Access**

Writ of Habeas Corpus: A signed document by a judge directing a child in a divorce or custody action be brought before the Court

APPENDIX D:

List of County Clerk's Offices

New York City Counties
Bronx County
851 Grand Concourse, Room 118
Bronx, New York 10451
866-797-7214

Kings County (Brooklyn)
360 Adams Street, Room 189
Brooklyn, New York 11201
347-404-9772

New York County (Manhattan)
60 Centre Street, Room 141B
New York, New York 10007
646-386-5955

Queens County
88-11 Sutphin Boulevard
Jamaica, New York 11435
718-298-0600

Richmond County (Staten Island)
130 Stuyvesant Place, 2nd Floor

Staten Island, New York 10301
718-675-7700

New York State Counties
Albany County
16 Eagle Street, Room 128
Albany, New York 12207
518-487-5100

Allegany County
7 Court Street, Room 18
Belmont, New York 14813
585-268-9270

Broome County
60 Hawley Street
PO Box 2062
Binghamton, New York 13902
607-778-2255

Cattaraugus County
330 Court Street
Little Valley, New York 14755
716-938-2297

Cayuga County
160 Genesee Street, 1st Floor
Auburn, New York 13021
315-253-1271

Chautauqua County
1 North Erie Street
PO Box 170
Mayville, New York 14757
716-753-4331

Chemung County
210 Lake Street
Elmira, New York 14901
607-737-2920

Chenango County
5 Court Street
Norwich, New York 13815
607-337-1450

Clinton County
137 Margaret Street, 1st Floor
Plattsburgh, New York 12901
518-565-4700

Columbia County
560 Warren Street
Hudson, New York 12534
518-828-3339

Cortland County
46 Greenbush Street, Suite 105
Cortland, New York 13045
607-753-5021

Delaware County
Court House Square
PO Box 426
Delhi, New York 13753
607-746-2123

Dutchess County
22 Market Street
Poughkeepsie, New York 12601
845-486-2120

Erie County
92 Franklin Street
Buffalo, New York 14202
716-858-8785

Essex County
7559 Court Street
Elizabethtown, New York 12932
518-873-3600

Franklin County
355 West Main Street, Suite 248
PO Box 70
Malone, New York 12953
518-481-1681

Fulton County
223 West Main Street
Johnstown, New York 12095
518-736-5555

Genesee County
15 Main Street
Batavia, New York 14020
858-344-2550, ext 2243

Greene County
411 Main Street
Catskill, New York 12414
518-719-3255

Hamilton County
Courthouse
PO Box 204 Route 8
Lake Pleasant, New York 12108
518-548-7111

Herkimer County
109 Mary Street, Suite 1111
Herkimer, New York 13350
315-867-1129

Jefferson County
175 Arsenal Street
Watertown, New York 13601
315-785-3081

Lewis County
7660 State Street
Lowville, New York 13367
315-376-5333

Livingston County
6 Court Street, Room 201
Geneseo, New York 14454
585-243-7010

Madison County
138 North Court Street
PO Box 668
Wampsville, New York 13163
315-366-2261

Monroe County
101 County Clerk's Office Building
39 West Maine Street
Rochester, New York 14614
585-753-1600

Montgomery County
64 Broadway
PO Box 1500

Fonda, New York 12068
518-853-8111

Nassau County
240 Old County Road
Mineola, New York 11501
516-571-2664

Niagara County
175 Hawley Street
PO Box 4561
Lockport, New York 14094
716-439-7022

Oneida County
800 Park Avenue
Utica, New York 13501
315-798-5794

Onondaga County
401 Montgomery Street, Room 200
Syracuse, New York 13202
315-435-2227

Ontario County
20 Ontario Street
Canandaigua, New York 14424
585-396-4200

Orange County
Parry Building
4 Glenmere Cove Road
Goshen, New York 10924
845-291-2690

Orleans County
3 South Main Street
Albion, New York 14411
585-589-5334

Oswego County
46 East Bridge Street
Oswego, New York 13120
315-349-8385

Otsego County
197 Main Street
PO Box 710
Cooperstown, New York 13326
607-574-4276

Putnam County
40 Gleneida Avenue
Carmel, New York 10512
845-225-3641, ext 300

Rensselaer County
105 Third Street
Troy, New York 12180
518-270-4080

Rockland County
1 South Main Street, Suite 100
New City, New York 10956
845-638-5070

Saratoga County
40 McMaster Street
Ballston Spa, New York 12020
518-885-2213

Schenectady County
620 State Street, 3rd Floor
Schenectady, New York 12305
518-388-4225

Schoharie County
PO Box 549
Schoharie, New York 12157
518-295-8316

Schuyler County
105 Ninth Street, Unit 8
Watkins Glen, New York 14891
607-535-8133

Seneca County
1 DiPronio Drive
Waterloo, New York 13165
315-539-1771

Saint Lawrence County
Building #2
48 Court Street
Canton, New York 13617
315-379-2237

Steuben County
3 East Pulteney Square
Bath, New York 14810
607-776-9631

Suffolk County
310 Center Drive
Riverhead, New York 11901
631-852-2000

Sullivan County
100 North Street
PO Box 5012
Monticello, New York 12701
845-807-0411

Tioga County
16 Court Street
PO Box 307
Owego, New York 13827
607-687-8660

Tompkins County
320 North Tioga Street
Ithaca, New York 14850
607-274-5431

Ulster County
244 Fair Street
PO Box 1800
Kingston, New York 12401
845-340-3000

Warren County
1340 State Route 9
Lake George, New York 12845
518-761-6429

Washington County
Municipal Center, Building A
393 Broadway
Fort Edward, New York 12828
518-746-2170

Wayne County
9 Pearl Street

PO Box 608
Lyons, New York 14489
315-946-7470

Westchester County
110 Dr. Martin Luther King Jr. Boulevard
White Plains, New York 10601
914-995-3080

Wyoming County
143 North Main Street, Suite 104
Warsaw, New York 14569
585-786-8810

Yates County
417 Liberty Street, Suite 1107
Penn Yan, New York 14527
315-536-5120

About the Author

An experienced litigator, **Brian D. Perskin, Esq.**, represents individuals in complex family and matrimonial law cases, including the negotiation and preparation of marital settlements, joint parenting plans, equitable distribution of assets, matters of custody and visitation, and prenuptial and postnuptial agreements.

Mr. Perskin has developed one of the largest matrimonial practices in the New York City area and is well respected amongst both his peers and judges as an aggressive advocate for men and women. The team at Brian D. Perskin & Associates P.C. is comprised of skilled, dedicated, and hardworking divorce and family law professionals. They are committed to the advancement of legal knowledge and use their extensive experience, skills, and legal expertise to advocate on their clients' behalves.

Mr. Perskin received his Bachelor of Arts degree in Economics from Brandeis University in 1987 and his Juris Doctor degree from Washington College of Law in 1990. He is admitted to practice in New York State and before the United States District Courts for the Southern and Eastern Districts.

Index